TESTIMONIAL
VOICES OF A
MOTHER

TESTIMONIAL VOICES OF A MOTHER

CHARLANDRA L. JACOBS

Scripture quotations are taken from the Holy Bible, King James Version, Cambridge, 1769. Used by permission. All rights reserved.

This book was Previously Published in 2014

ISBN: 978-1-09833-260-0

This book is printed on acid free paper.
Printed in the United States of America

This book is especially dedicated to my mother,
the late Jeanette Preston.

ACKNOWLEDGMENTS

First I would like to especially give thanks to my Heavenly Father for the grace that was bestowed upon me into writing this book. With God, all things are possible.

I would like to give special thanks to this great man of God, my best friend and my husband, Mr. Isaiah Jacobs II, for his infinite love and support. I love you so much, and you always tell me that God favored you when you married me, but God favored me as well.

I would like to acknowledge my pastors and my spiritual parents, Dr. Creflo Dollar and Pastor Taffi Dollar. They both have continuously imparted God's word with simplicity and understanding that has enhanced my God-given purpose in life.

I would like to acknowledge my mother's only sister, my beautiful aunt, Ms. Betty A. Johnson. She is a rock of motivation to us, as prayer warrior, and a bundle of love.

I would like to acknowledge my brother Edward Charles Pope Jr. and his beautiful family. My brother is a strong pillar and God-fearing man.

I would like to acknowledge my sister Jeanitris Pope-Cook and my brother-in-law Dr. Sean Cook. They are just a beautiful power couple of God.

Contents

INTRODUCTION

Testimonial Voices of a Mother is inspired by true life events about a God-fearing divorced single mother who believed in the power of prayer on a consistent basis. Also, she exemplified true Christian characteristics such as peace, longsuffering, meekness, temperance, and humility. I hope and pray that this book will minister to your heart, and be a great life-changing inspiration to you and your family.

BEGINNING YEARS

Growing up in Atlanta, Georgia, in the early 1970s as a little girl in a household of four was very challenging at times. Unfortunately, my parents divorced when I was approximately ten years old and it left a major negative impact on our household financially. My brother was about five years old and our baby sister was about one. My mother was a strong, loving woman and she raised us with God's strength.

Growing up, my mother had all of us on a routine schedule. For example, she would take all three of us to different schools using public transportation. By the time she arrived at her job, she was tired and sweaty, and she was exhausted when we were back at home for dinner. Unfortunately, there were times we had very little food to eat, but my mother would fast and sacrifice her appetite to make sure that my siblings and I had enough to eat for dinner. She would smile at us at times. She always believed God will always make a way of no way. Yes, despite the challenges, God still took care of us. Although we were forced to move several times, from public housing to living with relatives and sometimes to my mother's friends temporarily, my mother still continued to take us to church three times a week. I remember times when we would get home so late from church on a Friday night as well as staying at church all day on Sunday because we had limited transportation. On a Sunday night, we would arrive at home about 9:00 or 10:00 p.m. and my mother would start the routine all over again to prepare us for school the next day.

One time, there was an unfortunate experience while we were in transit to attend church services inside a public train station in Atlanta. Unfortunately, a faulty escalator caught my younger brother's pants, which ripped his pants and severely scratched and wounded his leg. My brother may have been around eight or nine years old at the time. My mother was very calm and focused and she immediately pulled my brother and called for help. Local train police who was nearby assisted us until an ambulance came and took us to a local hospital. My brother suffered severe bruises, but he recovered from them and my mother was compensated by public transportation services. My mother was able to purchase a reasonable car and of course she took care of her children. A great attribute about my mother is that she was always joyful in the midst of any problems.

She would always pray and encourage us that God would always take care of us and that everything will be all right. My mother usually meets me at the bus stop when I come from school. One particular day, she was not there. I got off the school bus and as soon as I got off, there were about three big, vicious, and scary dogs running toward me barking at me. Before the dogs came within steps of me, I saw a white figure that resembled a big angel come in front of me and I tried to look directly at it but the light was bright. Immediately the dogs turned away from me and ran away. I heard the angel say, "Don't be afraid. I will protect you." I then saw my mother coming to meet me. I ran and told her what just happened. She stated to me that she prayed to God to always protect me, my brother, and my sister. It made me think about that. I could have been seriously attacked, even killed, by those vicious dogs, but the prayers of my mother were so effective.

Even though my parents were divorced, my father was still present in our lives. He consistently picked us up on weekends and we would spend a lot of quality time with him. I would observe how my mother had always treated my father with respect in front of us. She has never said any negative words about my father. In addition, she would always teach us to respect my father and his new wife. My mother taught us that what so ever we sow with our words we will reap that and if you sow good words you will reap good words back in your life.

During my teenage years, I would stay with my father and his new wife and there were times I was mistreated and compared to my stepbrothers. My stepbrothers received favoritism at times when my father was at work and I would have to stay there with his wife. On the other hand, when I returned home, I would share those things with my mother and my mother would pray about it. My mother would continue to teach me how to continue to respect my stepmother and my father. Of course, my mother was intelligent to ensure that I was not physically abused or harmed. This was not the case. My mother always taught my siblings and me to always respect our elders, adults, teachers, and actually anybody that we come in contact with. God will always work every situation out. Also, my mother imparted words of wisdom in us. She would pray for God's perfect will to be upon us always and that we will grow up to be great men and women of God.

THE SECRET
MY MOTHER KEPT

My mother grew up in a home in Atlanta, Georgia, with only one younger sibling, my aunt Betty. They both lived with both parents in the household. My grandmother and my grandfather were hardworking people who raised two beautiful, young girls to become successful women. Growing up, my mother was always a woman who was very observant, wise, and did not express her feelings openly. Occasionally, my mother would share with me that growing up as a young girl in the fifties and sixties, she observed at times how her mother, my grandmother, would be treated unfairly and mentally abused by her father, my grandfather. Of course this abuse that she witnessed affected my mother psychologically. My grandmother would cry at times and try to stay strong for my mother and my aunt, but again she would consistently worry about her mother. Also, during that time, racism against black

Americans was still prevalent and there were times that my mother would observed a cross burning in her front yard or her parents being treated unfairly in a public store or restaurant. While attending high school in Atlanta, my mother was approached by several white girls and she was called racist names and bullied, but she told me that she got the strength from somewhere (God now) and defended herself and pushed a young lady's head down the toilet in the girl's restroom and left and started running.

When my mother graduated from high school, she decided to attend junior college and she got a job locally to be near my grandmother. On the other hand, when Aunt Betty graduated from high school, she got married and moved to Germany with her new husband. As the years passed, my mother met my father one day and they got married and eventually had three children. My father was a hardworking man and faithfully took care of his wife and children. One day, my mother was invited by one of her girlfriends to attend this church name Lakewood Church of God in Christ (COGIC) in Atlanta, Georgia. She decided to join this church and became a faithful member. Unfortunately, there were times that my father disagreed with how frequently my mother attended church, sometimes three to four times a week, and how she was required to pay large amounts of church dues, which affected their household income. This caused conflict and stress in the household. My parents ended up separating before my younger sister was born. Although my father moved on, he still spent time with his kids, took care of us, and was always in our lives while growing up. My mother was severely hurt and depressed on the inside, but she continued to cover up the hurt and raise her kids and love us unconditionally. During that time, my mother was pregnant with my younger sister. My father later married someone else and started a new family. The shocking secret was that my younger sister was born while my father just married someone else. Unfortunately, this bothered and hurt my mother for many, many years. She was such a strong woman of God and she continued to hide this inner hurt and raise her three children in the admonition of the Lord.

HEALING BATTLE

My mother moved my siblings and me to Decatur, Georgia, a suburban city of Atlanta. She found a very nice townhome for us to live in which was closer to her place of work. Unfortunately, this area became infested with crimes, drug dealers, and gangs. Throughout the neighborhood, my mother was highly respected by many of the so-called bullies. They would greet her and acknowledge us as her kids. They wouldn't let anybody harm us. Of course, my mother would say that the angels of God are always encamped about us and will protect us.

There were times when we would have a low supply of food and finances to pay our bills. My mother would find a way to help us feel better. If our lights were turned off, we would use candles or a flashlight for light. My mother mentioned to me a time that God told her to go into a store, but she did not have any money. She said someone walked up to her and gave her fifty dollars, saying God told him me to give her the money. She never saw that person again. Well, God blessed us again.

Also, my mother had such a big loving heart toward others. There was another time we were all at a store and my mother took her shoes off and gave her new pair of shoes to a lady who was barefoot. It was a beautiful thing for me to see my mom give someone in need a pair of shoes when my mother didn't have many shoes herself. I would see at many times the love of God demonstrated through my mother. My mother continued to work as an evangelist in the church and raise three beautiful children.

On one particular day, my siblings and I were in our room and we heard a loud boom, like someone had fallen in the kitchen. I ran toward the noise and my mother was on the kitchen floor and her eyes were white and she couldn't speak or move. I called 911 and of course my sister and brother were crying. When the ambulance came my mom was rushed to the hospital. Also, I called my aunts and my father and other relatives to come and meet us at the hospital. At the hospital, I overheard my mother's doctor speak to my aunt. The doctor said that my mother had a brain aneurysm and it was a blessing she was still alive, although they said that my mother would live to be a vegetable and her life span would be less than a year. They insisted that my mother should have surgery and there was no guarantee that she would be able to function normally. My mother stayed in the hospital several days.

Also, I remember in the hospital room my aunt, other relatives, and my spiritual grandparents, Bishop and Juanita Whitlock from the Lakewood church in Atlanta, Georgia, praying. They all prayed. After several more days, my mother became conscious. She told us, "The devil wants me off the face of the earth but God says I'm not going anywhere right now. I have too much work to do for God and my children need me." In days my mother was discharged from the hospital and several years went by and she still was doing great. This was again another miracle witnessed by doctors. In addition, this was a challenging time for me because I was occasionally dating a guy in high school that was jealous, controlling and abusive towards me.

While out on a date with him; he would take his frustration out on me and become very angry and upset if someone looks or stares at me. It was very embarrassing and hurtful. Later, he would apologize and change into a different person. We would become friends again. Of course, at this time in my life, my mother knew what was going on in my life and she disliked his ways; but she consistently prayed for me. I believe through my mother's prayers that things did not become worse in my life. For instance, there were many times you hear stories on the news that young women were killed as a result of domestic violence. I thank God for his grace and mercy. Although, I never told my father, because this would have upset him very bad and possibly he would have confronted my abusive boyfriend.

Unfortunately, my boyfriend at that time experienced serious issues with the law and in and out of jail, but for some reason I still loved him and we had dreams to get married and to start a new life together. Abuse is not love; it's only someone that is expressing their pain, guilt, and insecurity on someone else instead of getting the help that they need. At that time I didn't understand and I was very young and insecure and I didn't know that God wanted the best for me. Although, my boyfriend was very nice and brilliant young man; he was dealing with a lot of issues. His family so loving towards me and treated me special; but it's just that we were not compatible as a couple together for that time in my life. I prayed for him and I wished him and his family much success in their life ahead.

Well, thank God for my mother's prayers that he had a better plan for my life. As I began to have a close relationship with God, he revealed to me that the blessing of the Lord makes us rich and happy and it adds no sorrow. I realized that God loves us so much that he wants the best for me. In addition, it's God's perfect will that we have good, happy, and favorable relationships in our life. He desires that we prosper and have good health as our soul shall prosper too.

PRAYERS OF A MOTHER

After graduating from high school, I decided to visit New York City and stay with my aunt temporarily instead of attending college right away. After several months of living in New York City's fast life, I decided to go into the military and join the US Army.

While in the military, I faced many challenges of learning how to work in a diverse atmosphere and obtaining much more discipline that I encountered at home. When I successfully completed the US Army basic training course, I was on my way toward my military career.

While stationed in Ft. Lee, Virginia, near Petersburg, Virginia, I received PCS (Permanent Change of Station) orders to go to Korea. Of course, when you receive official orders as a soldier, you must obey and execute. On the other hand, personally, I did not want to go to Korea. At that time in the early nineties, there were serious economic and political issues going on. Well, I contacted my mother with the news about going to Korea and shared with her how

I felt. She told me as usual that she would pray for me and that God would work it out. Well, several days later, while I was still stationed at Ft. Lee, Virginia, my NCOIC (noncommissioned officer-in-charge) gave me new orders to Hawaii instead of Korea. Praise the Lord! I was so excited. Also, my NCOIC told me, "Soldier, I don't know where you come from, but things like this usually don't happen in the military. Somebody was praying for you."

Well, at the end of day, I called my mother back in Atlanta about the good news. Her voice was so calm over the phone as she said, "Pinky, I know. I prayed to God and he worked it out."

Well, my mother again was always a praying woman. She would encourage me that there was nothing too hard for God. This is true. "Is there anything too hard for the Lord?" (Genesis 18:4, KJV). "With men this is impossible; but with God all things are possible to him?" (Matthew 19:26, KJV).

As I prepared to transition to Hawaii from Ft. Lee, Virginia, I contacted my mother again and told her that as soon as I land in Hawaii, I would call her back to let her know how my flight was. According to my military orders, I was to report to active duty for three years on Schofield Barracks Army Base near Honolulu, Hawaii.

After one year of being stationed in Hawaii, I decided to visit my mother and family during the Christmas holidays. This particular time, I decided to surprise my mother. I asked my father to pick me up at the airport once I flew in to Atlanta. My father took me to my mom's townhouse and we saw her getting out of the car, but she didn't see me. I got out of my dad's car and I ran behind her and said, "Hi, Mom."

She turned around and dropped her bags and yelled, "Oh my God, Pinky! You're here." She was excited and happy. She had the biggest grin on her face. My mother always had beautiful teeth. We truly had a wonderful two weeks spent together.

After my visit, I reported back to active duty in Hawaii. Several months later, I got a call from my brother that my mother was sick. I was granted a military pass and I flew back to Atlanta. When I arrived, my mother was already in the hospital and I was anxious to find out from the doctors my mother's diagnosis.

When I was informed of my mother's illness and how serious it was, I contacted my commander in Hawaii and told him of my mother's condition. I requested a reassignment to be stationed at the nearest military base near my home to help take care of my mother, which was Ft. McPherson Army Base.

Unfortunately, my reassignment was disapproved and I was ordered to go back to Hawaii and finish my three-year tour. As I continued to complete my military tour in Hawaii, I had three special military buddies who prayed and supported me through thick and thin. Their names are

Angela Porter, Cheryl Henderson, and Lanora Wyatt. As of today, we are very close friends. Several months later, still in Hawaii, I received a phone call from my mother back in Atlanta. She was discharged out of the hospital and she encouraged me and said, "Don't worry about your reassignment being disapproved because God will turn it around for you." Also, she added, "Just look at it like this, you were only going back to Hawaii to prepare to pack your belongings." Well, after a couple of months in Hawaii, I got official orders that my reassignment was approved. I was so excited and many of my fellow soldiers and friends asked, "How did you get that to happen?" I just answered, "God did it just like my mother told me. She is truly a praying woman of God."

I was reassigned to Ft. McPherson, Georgia, and now working closer to home to check on my mother. After several months at my new station, I experienced harassment and unfair treatment from my company commander and my sergeant. Their hostile behavior toward me was so offensive and did not exemplify military values. As the days and months went by, the hostile and verbal harassment became worse. I decided to go and file a complaint with JAG, which is the military legal office. Well, the JAG office was already aware of the verbal harassment, because civilians who worked with me had already informed JAG about my unfair treatment. Overall, this negative treatment began to affect my confidence and brought about insecurities. I wanted to give up and go AWOL and just leave everybody. I felt like nobody knew what I was going through. Of course, I didn't want to bother my mother with my problem. As I was driving home one day in my car, I turned on the radio, which I usually don't listen to that much since I listen to CDs. Well, a song, "The Battle Is the Lord" by Yolanda Adams, came on the radio and the words caught my attention. I felt like Yolanda Adams and God was in my car and personally singing to me. As tears rolled down my ears, I felt like every heavy weight was lifted off of me and I was free from every burden. I knew at that moment what I was going through that it was over. Next, I heard a small voice say, "This battle is mine and not yours." I knew that voice was God's because I felt perfect peace and tranquility come over me. I was in a place of no lack, and I was made whole immediately.

Of course, the next day my company commander asked me in his office and stood in my face and yelled at me very loudly. He told me if I thought I could get out of anything. As a soldier, I felt like I had the strength of twenty men and his actions did not bother me anymore. The day before, I hid God's word in my heart and nothing could upset me. He released me and I left his office. Within a week, my company commander was relieved and along with my NCOIC sergeant. They were both reassigned out of the country.

I called my mother to tell her the good news and how I learned to trust that God would work my situation out. Furthermore, she began to tell me that God had already revealed to her what I was going through. Also, she said, "Remember I told you that our battles are God's battles and he fights them for us." She said that God loved us and that's why he gave us his son Jesus. Also, she told me to remember that what the devil meant for bad God will always turn around for good. Again, my mother, the encourager. She was a woman who always saw sunshine in the midst of any turmoil.

The next day at work, I was promoted within the military and transferred to a much better organization and I received my good conduct medal award. God is so faithful and he really does fight our battles for us.

One day my mother called me to tell me that someone had broken into her townhouse when she was not at home and stole some things that were valuable to us and ransacked the place. I immediately went to see her townhome. It was a total mess. They stole valuable items such as the TV and stereo, and the large woodcraft Hawaiian clock I bought her while stationed in Hawaii. My mother was staying with relatives. Her spirit was so calm and peaceful. She was a woman who always cast her cares on God and prayed for her children. At that time, I was still staying in the military base at Ft. McPherson. I told my mother not to worry about anything and that I will purchase her a house. The next week, I contacted a real estate agent and expressed my interest in wanting to purchase a house. I was told by others about my decision to buy a house, "You are too young to purchase your own house at twenty-one-years old," or "You can buy yourself a condo for yourself." I ignored their comments and I trusted God along with my mother. I found a beautiful house in suburban Atlanta that I was able to afford. Furthermore, I closed on my new home in thirty days. I called my mother because she was still staying with a relative. I told my mother to pack her bags and come and move into her new house. Although I purchased the home, it was actually for my mother. Praise God I was able to purchase a five-bedroom and three-bath brick house for my mother and my two siblings. God is such an awesome God. My mother has always told us, "With God all things are possible to him that believes" (Matthew 19:26, KJV).

God's Purpose
for My Mother
Is Greater than Life
on This Earth

As years passed, my mother continued to enjoy living in her new home and working in the church ministry. She would both work at her physical job as a social worker and work as a minister and speak at churches and visit hospitals and nursing homes to pray for others. She was always putting others before herself. I would come home and see her tired body and suggest that she rest.

One day, when I came home and my younger brother was there, we heard a loud noise in my mother's bedroom. We rushed in and my mother was on her knees in her room and she couldn't get up. My brother and I began to feel this violent rush of wind and anger in the room from another force. My brother and I begin to get on our knees along with my mother and we prayed. We prayed and prayed. I remember my mother taught us at a young age about God's war angel, Michael. I begin to call Michael the war angel to come and fight this battle. I spoke over my mother, "No weapon formed against you shall prosper in Jesus's name." In minutes, my mother stood up and my brother and I got up and hugged her. The rooms immediately began to be filled with peace and joy. Our eyes were teary and we saw angels of God fill the room and we begin to praise God. That was my second time witnessing God's angels. Later, my mother had shared with us that she was sick and she felt that the devil was trying to attack her body. She blessed God for having a daughter and son to pray over her. My mother had imparted in us that prayer changes things.

I asked her if she would like for me to still take her to the doctor and get checked out. Although we prayed spiritually, we still wanted her to be examined physically. After her doctor's appointment, she was advised by her physician to rest.

As a soldier, I had the option to reenlist, receive an honorable discharge and leave the military, or join the Army Reserves. I knew if I reenlisted, I would probably be reassigned out of the country or to another destination. I decided to receive an honorable discharge and leave active duty and join the Army Reserves. Also, I received a civilian job working at the base.

One day, my mother and I were talking in the kitchen. "Pinky" was my nickname my dad and my mom gave me. She said, "Pinky, God is going to bless you with a husband that loves God and will love you unconditionally." Also, she told me that God was going to bless my younger brother and sister with mates as well. She told me that she had seen all of us already married and she saw her beautiful grandchildren. Of course, I was a little uncomfortable when my mother talked this way because I was thinking that she was planning on going somewhere, but she was a woman of great faith and God's wisdom.

Several months came by, on one particular day, I came home to find my mother lying down in our family room and unresponsive. I called 911 and the ambulance arrived and picked her up. Of course, I didn't want to believe the worst, but I knew instantly that my mother had passed away before she arrived at the hospital. While at the hospital with family and friends, the physician came out and gave us the terrible news. I felt like my whole world caved in. I felt so empty and bad, like someone had pierced my heart. On the other hand, I had to keep a strong spirit for my younger brother and sister.

I asked God, "How am I going to get through this?" I told God this was too hard for me to handle. "I don't understand," I said to God. "Why did my mother pass away so soon?"

During my mother's home-going service, it was truly a celebration and not a sad occasion. My father was there to support us. My father had always been a part of our lives. I had never seen so many people say good things about my mother. In fact, some of the people were strangers to me. A young pastor walked up to me and said, "Out of all the home-going services that I've been too, I've never seen one like this." He saw angels rejoicing all over the church and he told me, "I can't say this about everybody but there is no doubt or question in my heart that your mother is truly in heaven rejoicing with the angels in Gods' presence."

Also, one of my close friends told me, "You are a very strong woman because I would have lost my mind if my mother would have died. I couldn't have handled it."

Over the next couple of days, I still felt very sad about my mother passing. On the other hand, she lived nearly ten years longer than her physicians predicted and that was a miracle by itself, but then again, when the service was over and days have gone by and everyone was gone, I was still at home alone, I still had questions, and I didn't understand why so soon.

One night, I went to bed and I had an interesting dream. In my dream, I felt peace, joy, and happiness. I saw gold streets and gigantic beautiful houses that look like castles. These homes were nothing like the billion-dollar custom-made homes on earth. I saw angels singing and praising God. I walked into one of the homes and I saw my mother but she had a new body and I saw a crown with precious jewels on her head. These jewels seemed more valuable than any piece of jewel I have ever seen. Although my mother did not recognize me as her daughter, she had this big gigantic smile on her face and she was rejoicing and praising God with the angels. She was so happy and free and the atmosphere was full of peace. I saw Jesus and I touched him but he had a new body as well.

I heard the voice of God tell me, "It was your mother's desire to come to heaven and be in my presence so soon. I gave your mother her heart's desire and I promised her that I will take care of you and your brother and your sister forever and ever."

I woke up from the dream, but of course I didn't want to wake at all. It felt so good to be in God's presence that I didn't want to come out of it. Again, as I woke up, I had so much peace and understanding about my mother's sudden death. God truly gave me understanding. Although I took it one day at a time, I began to rely on God more and more and I was totally convinced that the joy of the Lord is my strength. God was the only one who could reveal to me understanding about my mother's death. Although my mother was young and close to fifty when she passed away and went home to be with the Lord, she gained Godly wisdom and used it while she lived on this earth. I believe that God desires for us to have long life on this earth, but now my mother has eternal life in the presence of God.

THE DATING LIFE
AS A CHRISTIAN WOMAN

Dating as a single Christian Woman was not easy but with God all things are possible to him that believes. I allowed this word to root in my heart and I remembered my mother's words to me one day, "Daughter, I desire that you, your brother, and your sister will marry someone that loves God wholeheartedly and will love you like Jesus Christ loves the church." I received that word from my mother and I prayed to God and asked him to send me a husband that loves you and will love me unconditionally.

Also, loving God with all of your heart makes it so much easier to date because it's about pleasing God and yourself or your body. There were many times that I was attracted to handsome men in my life, and I would go out on a date. Some of these men would be attracted to me sexually, but of course, I would always suggest that I would rather wait until I get married before I have sex because I love my body and it is the temple of the Holy Spirit. A person with charm may desire to take advantage of you or speak enticing words to pursue their motive for a moment without a commitment. On the other hand, a person with character may give the advantage to others, and respect your wishes and desires, and compliment you without a price or a bad motive. Ultimately they may desire a long-term commitment with you. Yes, I am aware that some Christians are going to make mistakes in life. As a Christian woman, I made some mistakes, and I've learned from those mistakes. One of the best advantages of being a born-again believer is that you have the Holy Spirit to help you, and although he will convict you of any bad mistakes, he will still guide you in continuous right standing with God. Thank God for great grace and mercy, and there is no condemnation to those that are in Christ Jesus.

Another thing I learned while dating as a Christian is that the Holy Spirit will direct you as who to date as well certain environments that may or may not be beneficial to your spirit. For example, I decided not to go to nightclubs or attend lustful parties because I wanted to protect my relationship with God and I wanted to attract a man of God with a fulfilling purpose.

I would like to share this with single women or men today who desire to be married or to have a prosperous relationship. Honor and receive God's word about relationships. Amos 3:3 states that, "Can two walk together, except they be agreed?" For instance, I believe that if you and your partner don't agree on spiritual things, how do you expect to agree on natural things? It's very important to have a close relationship with God and allow the Holy Spirit to lead and guide you. As humans, we have the tendency to choose relationships with our eyes first. Of course it's good to want someone who looks good on the outside, but get to know their spirit first and find out their motives and their heart's desire before you become intimate with them. For instance, if you become intimate with them first then strong soul ties will begin to develop and become stronger and then you become off focus on your spiritual connection. We are human individuals and that's why in my opinion people should wait on becoming intimate first, because it's more beneficial for a relationship to be drawn spiritually together first, and then the both of you can allow God to do what he needs to do in order to grow that relationship in a positive way. Work on becoming friends, because a true friend will give the advantage and not take the advantage from you. They will love and not pressure you to compromise your values or beliefs.

Especially as women, we are emotional, strong, and special human beings who desire to be loved unconditionally. The good news is that this is God's will as he loves us unconditionally and he wants us to have healthy and Godly relationships. On the other hand, we must allow God to help us by submitting to his way.

Furthermore, my family and I were preparing to have my mother's home-going service, we were taking it one day at a time. Without my mother and my best friend, it was not easy at all. I thank God for my aunt and my mother's only sister, Betty A. Johnson. She was always a rock of support for us financially and spiritually. Per my mother's instructions before her death, she mentioned to me several times to ensure that her life insurance policy was active. My mother was always correct and on point about things and she saw things before they would manifest. Unfortunately, I procrastinated and did not follow up to ensure that her life insurance policy was still active. Therefore, we did not have sufficient funds to pay for her burial expenses. As the eldest child, this became very stressful for me and I condemned and blamed myself for this mistake. During my prayer time with God, he began to minister to me and he said, "Daughter, cast all of your cares on me because I care for you and I love you. I promised your mother that I will take care of you and your brother and sister always as long you all continue to trust in me. I am your God." Again, I always felt strength in God. As favor with God, the funeral home allowed us to proceed with my mother's burial with the full burial package and gave us an estimated time to pay the expenses. She was laid to rest in the best. We had an awesome home-going service and I saw a vision of the angels from heaven singing and rejoicing in the church. What a time of celebration we had.

About a week after the service, I received a very large check in the mail enough to not only pay for my mother's burial expenses, but there it was money left over for me to bless my brother and my sister financially. The check was retroactive back pay from a military settlement that I was waiting on and I was told that this settlement could take several years, but God's timing is not man's timing and God did just what he said he would do. I would still encourage others to make sure that your business affairs are in order such as life insurance policies for your loved ones and family. It's very important to ensure that your affairs are in place in case something happens like a death in the family.

HE WHO FINDS A WIFE
FINDS A GOOD THING

As months went by, I continued to be faithful to God and I decided to become a prayer volunteer at Trinity Broadcasting Network. TBN is one of the world's largest Christian television networks. After work, I would go and volunteer at the TBN satellite office in Decatur, Georgia. My experience working as a prayer volunteer was so powerful. It was a privilege to pray for people all over the world. For instance, my problems would become nonexistent and my focus would be totally on God's mission for his kingdom. As a result, many souls would become born again, healed, delivered, and restored. To God be the glory.

On one occasion, en route to my home, I visited a store to purchase some items. While in line, there was a handsome, muscular guy behind me. He asked for some directions. I thought he was going to ask for my name or something. I guess that burst my bubble. Anyway, I gave him the information he asked for, and before I realized it, we began talking about the military. At that time, I was still an active Army reservist and he was an Army veteran. He began to share with me about how God has led him to come to Georgia, but he wasn't sure what the purpose was yet. I invited him to my church and we exchanged phone numbers. He was so handsome and such a gentlemen, Lord help me that day. After many months of dating, I invited him to dinner at my home with friends and family. Although I wasn't much of a good cook in his opinion, he proposed to me and told me, "Now I understand why I am in Georgia. God sent me here to find my wife and it's you. Will you marry me?" I accepted. We decided to stay in separate homes until we got married the next year and as of today we have three beautiful children.

At that time, my husband and I were members of another local church in the Atlanta area, although I began to feel that God was leading us into a different direction about a new church home. Therefore, we decided to visit World Changers Church International. After several visits, I wanted to tell my husband that God had placed in my heart to join this church, but I was hoping God would reveal to him the same thing. So, I decided to share with him the good news about joining this church. My husband replied, "Let's join this church."

We prayed together and asked God, "Is this your will God?"

God said yes to our spirits, that it was his will for us to join this church. My husband and I immediately joined World Changers and accepted to partake in the vision of our spiritual leaders, Dr. Creflo Dollar and Pastor Taffi Dollar. At this moment, I knew that my mother was smiling down from heaven on us. God is awesome always.

REAPING THE HARVEST

There was another time in my life that I was experiencing severe verbal harassment and workplace bullying from a former supervisor. For example, I was verbally harassed and embarrassed and belittled in front of coworkers. The devils began to bring fear to me about losing my job because I was a new employee. I couldn't speak up or tell somebody about my concerns. As months went by, I would continue to experience this unprofessional behavior and harassment from my supervisor. Unfortunately, I wanted to give up and quit because at this point I hated to come to work. Also, the commute to this job was ninety miles one way. One day, when I came home after work, my husband began to pray for me and encourage me, telling me God has not given me the spirit of fear, but he has given me power love and a sound mind (2 Timothy 1:7, KJV). "Always know that the Joy of the Lord is my strength and not to Cast not away therefore your confidence, which hath great recompense of reward…this hath great recompense of reward" (Hebrews

10:35). No weapon formed against me shall prosper and every tongue that rises against me is condemned. It's a blessing to have a spouse who walks in the spirit when you are going through a bad situation. Also, I remember during service when Pastor Dollar was speaking about God's grace being sufficient to sustain us in the midst of every challenge and battle we face. The devil can only succeed in our life if we allow him too. Submit yourself to God and the devil will flee. God's ability is his grace.

Furthermore, as a federal employee, we had the opportunity to apply for job transfers nationwide. I began to apply for jobs and request a transfer closer to home in the Atlanta area within the federal government. Shortly, I was called on a job interview. During the interview, I was informed that 133 people were qualified, but only twenty-five applicants were referred and I was chosen to be interviewed.

After my job interview, I continued to work at my current job and waited patiently on the status of that job interview. Several months went by, then one day at work, God instructed me to ask my supervisor if I could talk to her. Of course, it wasn't easy to talk to her because of the unprofessional treatment that I have experienced from her. I submitted to and obeyed God. Also, I remembered my pastor Dr. Dollar mentioning that a humble man is the one who submits to the will of God and God gives grace to the humble and he will oppose the proud and exalt the person who walks in humility.

During my conversation with my supervisor, the presence of God came over us like a blanket of peace and love. We talked about things of God and I prayed for my manager and her family and that the blessings of God will overtake her household. Within a week, in December 2012, I got a call and I was given a job offer and I accepted. The bonus is that this new job will be located in Atlanta, Georgia. I no longer had to commute to work and drive ninety miles one way. Furthermore, I received two financial increases. God is faithful. Praise God!

The word of God says, "There is nothing too hard for God and with God all things are possible to him that believeth"(Mark 9:23).

AUTHOR'S NOTES

I desire that this book will be an encouragement to those that has had family members or friends that have gone home to be with The Lord. We sometimes don't understand "Why did this happen?" or "Why did God allow this to happen?. I know that I felt that way when my mother passed away to glory. God was the only one that can answer my questions and fill that void. God was and still is my perfect that surpasses all understanding. Hopefully this book will be a life changer and minister to your heart and spirit. Always remember to walk in Godly love quickly, forgive others, and always put your trust in God and not man.

If you are not born again, I invite you to become born again today. Please repeat, "Heavenly Father, I repent from my sins. Come into my life and save me." "If thou shall confess with thy mouth the Lord Jesus, and shall believe in thine heart that God hath raised him from the dead, thou shalt be saved" (Roman 10:9).

Now continue to grow in God's will and his blessings for your life. If you received this prayer you are born again and a new creature in Christ. "Therefore if any man be in Christ, he is a new creature old things are passed away and behold all things are become new" (Corinthians 5:17).

Now continue in God's will and his eternal blessings for your life. Congratulations, you are spirit-filled and born again and a winner in Christ Jesus always.

ABOUT THE AUTHOR

Mrs. Charlandra Latrice Jacobs is a native of Atlanta, Georgia. She is a wife, mother, author, co-owner of J'Naruci men's clothing wear, and upcoming actress. She lives in suburban Atlanta, Georgia, with her husband and children. Charlandra and her family are faithful members of World Changers Church International founded by Dr. Creflo Dollar and his wife, Pastor Taffi Dollar.

Charlandra received her high school diploma from Columbia High School in Decatur, Georgia. Also, she is a US Army veteran, she received an honorable discharge, and she is a recipient of the Good Conduct Medal. She attended Troy State University and Saint Leo University where she received an associates degree, bachelor's degree in accounting, and her master's degree in business administration.

As a co-owner with her husband of the new and upcoming luxury clothing brand, J'Naruci, their vision was to start a luxury clothing brand for men to dress for success, distinction, and style.

For her first book, *Testimonial Voices of a Mother*, Charlandra desired to write inspiring and uplifting messages from her own personal testimonies and challenges. Charlandra is known for being featured in the TV One film, *A Christmas Blessing*. Also, she appeared in a featured role in the Lifetime movie, *The Trip to Bountiful*, starring Cicely Tyson and Blair Underwood. Also, Charlandra played background roles in Tyler Perry's *The Haves and the Have Nots and Love Thy Neighbor* on the OWN network, as well as many other future film projects. Also, she has appeared in a commercial as one of the spokespersons for Jim Ellis Automotive Group in the metro Atlanta area.

As a motivational speaker, Charlandra has spoken at several local churches to encourage others about God's successful plan for their lives. Also, she was guest speaker for the Dr. Betty Shabazz Delta Sigma Theta foundation to inspire young black girls that they rock and that they are beautiful inside and out and that they can achieve success with the right mindset. She is continuing to speak and inspire young kids at local schools and charities and to inspire others to never let their dream die and that God loves them no matter what and that he has a successful plan for their lives, but their words are the seeds that will determine the outcome.

Charlandra has a younger brother who is married with four beautiful children and lives in South Carolina. He and his wife are entrepreneurs with a successful business and ministering together in their local church and loving God wholeheartedly.

Also, she has a younger sister who is married and lives in Atlanta Georgia with her loving husband. They are youth pastors, professional gospel singers, and loves God unconditionally.

Charlandra encourages you to know that God has a successful plan for your life; your words are seeds, and they will determine your outcome. Always remember that God loves you no matter what and that he wants to do you good all the time. God desires that you live the good life forever. Be blessed.